Swing Classics

BENNY GOODMAN CLARINET SOLOS

with piano accompaniment

Solo			Piano
Air Mail Special	2	1	Air Mail Special
Grand Slam	4	4	Grand Slam
Gone With What Draft	6	7	Gone With What Draft
Flying Home	8	9	Flying Home
Mission To Moscow	10	11	Mission To Moscow
Benny's Bugle	12	15	Benny's Bugle

T0045113

Air Mail Special

By Benny Goodman,
Jimmy Mundy
and Charlie Christian

CLARINET

Bright Tempo

3

Grand Slam

CLARINET *Boogie Woogie Style*

By Benny Goodman

Gone With What Draft

CLARINET

Medium Bounce

By Benny Goodman

Air Mail Special

By Benny Goodman,
Jimmy Mundy
and Charlie Christian

PIANO

1

3

Grand Slam

Boogie Woogie Style
PIANO

By Benny Goodman

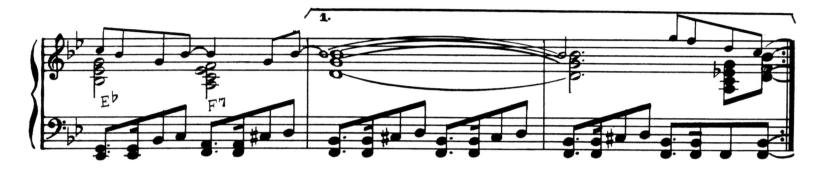

Gone With What Draft

By Benny Goodman

PIANO

Medium Bounce

Flying Home

By Benny Goodman
and Lionel Hampton

PIANO   *Medium Bounce*

9

Mission To Moscow

By Mel Powell

PIANO

13

Benny's Bugle

PIANO

By Benny Goodman

Moderato

16

PLAY 3 TIMES (*p*, *mf*, *ff*)

Flying Home

CLARINET

By Benny Goodman
and Lionel Hampton

Goodman Solo

Mission To Moscow

By Mel Powell

CLARINET

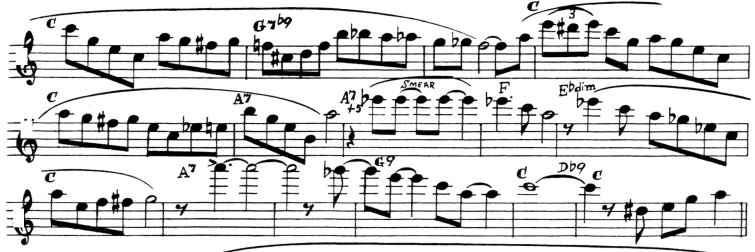

Benny's Bugle

By Benny Goodman

CLARINET
Moderato